Lincoln's Table

Abraham Lincoln (artist unknown) and Mary Todd Lincoln, painted by Katherine Helm.
(Townsend Collection of Mary Genevieve Townsend Murphy)

Lincoln's Table

Victorian Recipes from Kentucky, Indiana, and Illinois to the White House

❦

Donna D. McCreary

Guild Press of Indiana, Inc.

GUILD PRESS OF INDIANA, INC.
10665 Andrade Drive
Zionsville, Indiana 46077
317-733-4175

ISBN 1-57860-089-8

Front cover: A tea service in the dining room of the Lincoln Home National Historic Site in Springfield, Illinois. *Back cover*: Mary Todd Lincoln learned to cook on a stove like the one featured here, also in the Lincoln Home, producing some of her specialties, such as the White Almond Cake (shown in the inset).

Tea service and stove photos courtesy Lincoln Home National Historic Site in Springfield, Illinois. Photos of Abraham and Mary Todd Lincoln are from the author's collection. Photo of Donna D. McCreary by Lori Reeder of Moments Photography, Charlestown, Indiana.

*Lovingly dedicated to
Elizabeth Ann Bruce Ellis,
who taught me the most important
ingredient is always love.*

Contents

Introduction and Acknowledgments

WHY A LINCOLN COOKBOOK? The man was a fussy eater and had no interest in food. After his death, Sally Lincoln, his stepmother said, "Abe was a moderate eater and I now have no remembrance of his special dish: he sat down and ate what was set before him, making no complaint." Others said that he ate only to live, and sometimes only when he was reminded to do so. Many historians have reported that he ate merely a poached egg for breakfast, an apple for lunch, and little if anything for supper. However, most historians are examining a fragment of his life, the presidential years, or basing their account of his eating habits on one comment from one person. Truthfully, Lincoln was a thin man; his weight was about one hundred and eighty pounds stretched over his six-foot, four-inch body when he entered the White House. Due to the stress and strain of the war, by its end, twenty pounds had vanished from his frame. So why a Lincoln cookbook?

Because, despite popular belief, Lincoln enjoyed good food.

Nathaniel Hawthorne had a nine A.M. appointment to meet the President. Not wanting to disrupt the President's schedule, Mr. Hawthorne was punctual. Lincoln was not. The President sent word to his waiting guest that he was having his breakfast. Hawthorne wrote, "His appetite, we were glad to think, must have been a pretty fair one; for we waited about half an hour in one of the antechambers."

Lincoln's Table

Lincoln's appetite indeed was a "fair one" as Hawthorne commented. Lincoln may have been extremely thin in 1865, but earlier in his life he had been described as fleshy, and muscular. In New Salem, Lincoln's weight was at least two hundred and twenty pounds, and was probably near that during his early years as a Springfield lawyer. Lincoln's cousin, John Hanks, who had lived with the Lincoln family for a four-year period in Indiana, commented, "Abraham was a good and hearty eater—loved good eating. His own mother and stepmother were good cooks for them days and times." Perhaps that is why Sally Lincoln never heard Abraham complain about food. The lad knew whatever was set before him would be tasty and enjoyable. In fact, as an adult, Lincoln often commented on several foods that he enjoyed: the Vanilla Almond Cake that Mary baked on special occasions, corn cakes, lemon pie, potatoes, and fruit. When traveling the circuit, if he especially enjoyed a dish at a boarding house, Lincoln would ask the proprietor for the recipe and then take it home to Mary. Lincoln did some of the grocery shopping in Springfield, carefully selecting the meat for the evening meal. In Washington, his interest and care about food almost completely disappeared. However, he did plan the menu for his first inaugural luncheon, and in the presence of visiting family members, especially early in his first term, he always ate a hearty breakfast.

But still, why a Lincoln cookbook?

Because, as I have learned, "performing is so portable."

One can take it wherever and whenever, and develop it how ever one desires. The living history program, "Love is Eternal—Mrs. Lincoln," is no exception. Throughout the years, the program has evolved to meet the needs of classroom teachers and students. It has developed and defined its own personality to become flexible for audiences of all ages. It was from the program's growth, that this cook book project started.

As I travel to various schools performing as Mrs. Lincoln, on occasion, someone will ask me if I had any recipes for "something Lincoln ate" or "something Mary cooked." I began searching for such recipes, and the first one I found was the above-mentioned Vanilla Almond Cake. I stumbled

upon an old copy of Poppy Cannon's *The Presidents' Cookbook*, and found a
few more things the Lincolns enjoyed while living in Washington, D.C. As
my recipe collection grew, so did the requests from schools. Instead of asking
for just one recipe, though, teachers began asking for menus to prepare for
special luncheons. They want desserts and beverages to serve at Victorian tea
parties. Some students have even organized "Lincoln baking contests" while
others organize Lincoln or Civil War bake sales. The enthusiasm of the
students and their teachers has encouraged me to continue searching for
more recipes.

This is a collection of recipes, each one of which has been traced to
Lincoln's dining table at some point in his life. That table may have been the
rough table made by his father, or the beautiful elaborate dining table used
for state dinners in the White House. Some recipes were enjoyed by the
Lincoln family in Springfield. Others were relished in fine New York
restaurants, the homes of friends, or boarding houses where Lincoln stayed
when he was a circuit lawyer. They all share one common thread—Lincoln
enjoyed them.

Many have helped gather information for this book, and I am greatly
indebted to them for their assistance. Several members of the Association of
Lincoln Presenters offered assistance with finding information, recipes,
photographs, research, and even taste-testing. Dan Bassuk, Murray Cox,
Max and Donna Daniels, Robert Henderson, Cliff and Joan Howard,
Patrick McCreary, Jim and Mary Sayre, and Macon and Linda Ray were
invaluable to the completion of this book. Fritz Klein provided motivation,
support, and some of the wonderful White House menus. Valerie Gugala
was a wonderful, energetic research assistant. William Ciampa of Abe's
Antiques of Gettysburg allowed me to use photos from his private collection
and provided a wonderful photo opportunity. Staff members from several
historic sites were helpful in assisting with information and validation of
stories about Lincoln family members and their life styles. A complete list
can be found in the bibliography of this book.

Family members and friends also helped with this project. My mother,

Lincoln's Table

Helen McCreary, makes the best pies this side of heaven, and she offered advice and her expertise with many of the recipes in this collection. Pam Beaufait allowed me to peruse her antique cookbook collection. Gerald D. Swick was there from the beginning offering research assistance, advice, and moral support. I am grateful to the late Mary Genevieve Townsend Murphy for the loan of her photo collection. Also helping from the inception was Greta Ratliff who aided with every phase of this project from providing information about historic cooking and recipes to testing recipes.

Finally, thanks to my publisher, Nancy Niblack Baxter, and editor and book designer, Sheila Samson, at Guild Press of Indiana for everything—they have given me the support and encouragement to complete the task.

Donna McCreary
October 2000

❧❀❧

Kentucky

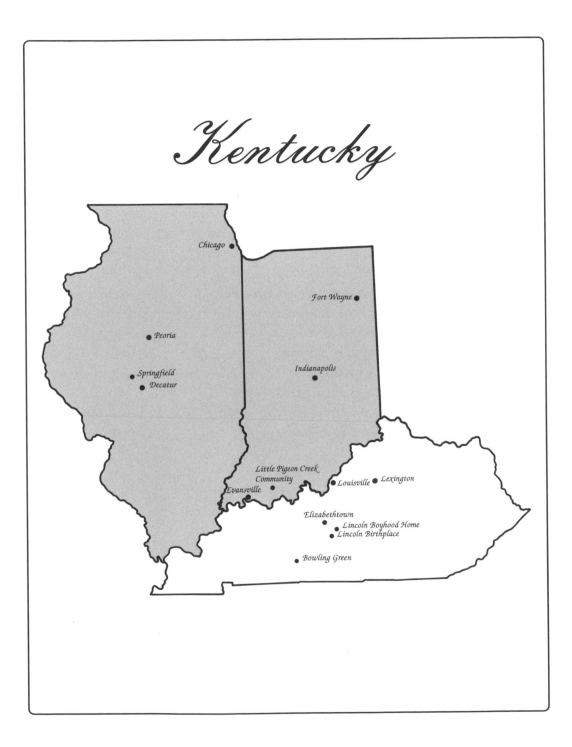

Chicago

Fort Wayne

Peoria

Indianapolis

Springfield
Decatur

Little Pigeon Creek
Community
Evansville

Louisville   Lexington

Elizabethtown
Lincoln Boyhood Home
Lincoln Birthplace

Bowling Green

When Thomas Lincoln married Nancy Hanks, Kentucky was the frontier. A family forged a living from the rich soil, growing crops, raising some domestic animals, and hunting wild animals and fowl for food. It was a difficult life, but it was a good life for the Lincoln family and their Kentucky neighbors. Little is known about what the Lincoln family ate during the years they lived in Kentucky. Most all early cookbooks and family domestic books included recipes for preparing wild game such as deer, pheasant, turkey, quail, rabbit, squirrel, woodchuck, and even bear. The Lincoln family would have eaten some, if not all, of the various types of wild game available in the area. Presumably, Thomas Lincoln and his son went fishing. Nancy tended a garden, and the woods were full of wild berries, persimmons, cherries, pawpaws, and nuts.

In addition to feeding the adults, Nancy Lincoln had to feed her children, Sarah and Abraham.

Abraham Lincoln lived two places in Kentucky. The first was known as the Sinking Spring farm, located near Hodgenville. Thomas Lincoln had purchased the 348½ acres for cash in December of 1808, and with his wife, Nancy, and their daughter, Sarah, moved to the farm. On February 12, 1809, Abraham was born. For two years, Thomas Lincoln worked the land only to discover the man who sold him the property did not have clear title to it. The Lincoln family then moved to the Knob Creek farm a few miles away. Later, Lincoln wrote that his first memories were of the Knob Creek farm. It was here that he first remembered eating corn cakes for breakfast. Often, he joked that he could "eat corn cakes twice as fast an anyone could make them." They continued to be his favorite breakfast and late Sunday supper dish throughout his life.

These are delicious with butter and maple syrup. Lincoln ate them drenched in sorghum syrup and butter. These are best when eaten hot off the griddle, and a cold glass of buttermilk makes them even more Lincolnesque.

Knob Creek Kentucky Corn Cakes

(Makes 32–36 two-inch cakes)

2	cups cornmeal
1	teaspoon salt
1	teaspoon soda
1	egg, lightly beaten
3	cups buttermilk

Sift together cornmeal, salt, and soda. Add the egg and buttermilk. Mix well to blend, but do not overbeat. (The batter should be thin enough to form a lacy edge when baking.) Drop by small spoonfuls on a hot griddle; cook till golden, turn, and finish cooking. Stack cakes on a cookie sheet and place in a 250 degree oven to keep warm.

Cooking with a Dutch oven—a deep metal pot with a close-fitting lid—is still popular. Iron cookware is used by campers, re-enactors, and by outdoor enthusiasts. Proper care must be used to maintain these essential cooking utensils.

Before using a piece of iron cookery, it must be properly seasoned. This is done by rubbing lard, shortening, or beef suet over the entire surface of the inside of the pot. Place it in an oven at 150 degrees and leave for two hours. Prepare the outside of the pot in the same manner, and again, return to the oven for two hours. Remove from the oven, and allow the item to cool. Wash with warm, soapy water and dry well. Return the pot to the oven to dry (drying beside a campfire is often recommended).

After using an iron pot, wash it with warm, soapy water, and scrub well. Dry thoroughly either by hand, or by placing near a fire or in an oven. Never leave water standing in an iron pot—rust will ensue. And never store an iron Dutch oven with its lid in place, or it will acquire a musty odor, trap moisture, and develop rust spots.

The Lincoln family would have enjoyed a mug of buttermilk with these potatoes, thus making a hearty meal.

Nancy Hanks' Steamed Potatoes

(Serves 6–10)

6 to 10 medium-sized
    potatoes
1 cup water
  Salt and pepper
  Butter

Scrub potatoes well. Pile into an iron Dutch oven. Pour salted water over potatoes. Place the lid on the Dutch oven. On top of the lid, place several pieces of glowing charcoal or embers from a fire. (If cooking in a modern oven, preheat the oven to about 300 degrees.)

Steam potatoes slowly for about an hour or until they are tender. Do not lift the lid unless absolutely necessary. Serve potatoes in their jackets with salt, pepper, and butter.

This cake is served without icing. It is wonderful with a little powdered sugar sprinkled on the top, or served with whipped cream or ice cream.

Sorghum Cake

(serves 8–10)

½   cup butter
1   cup sugar
1   slightly beaten egg
1   cup sorghum
3 ½ to 3 ¾ cups sifted flour
¼   teaspoon nutmeg
¼   teaspoon cinnamon
1   teaspoon baking soda
1   teaspoon baking powder
1   cup sour milk

Grease and flour a 13 x 9-inch cake pan. Preheat oven to 325 degrees.

Cream together butter and sugar. Slowly add the slightly beaten egg and sorghum. Beat mixture well. Sift all the dry ingredients together. Alternately add dry ingredients and the milk to the creamed mixture. When all ingredients are added, beat well. Pour batter into prepared pan and bake about 40–45 minutes, or until cake tests done. (This cake can also be baked in a bread pan, or a bundt cake pan. In such a case, increase the baking time to one hour.)

Proper Food for Children

Sarah Josepha Hale was a well-known writer during the nineteenth century. She was the editor of *Godey's Ladies Magazine* and was a leading factor in women's fashion, health, and social reform, known by almost every woman in American, and even by some men, including Abraham Lincoln. Hale is remembered today as the author of the poem "Mary Had a Little Lamb."

In her articles and books, Hale wrote to young mothers and new housekeepers. In the following excerpt from her book, *The Good Housekeeper*, published in 1841, are Hale's guidelines for ensuring good nutrition for children.

The milk of the mother ought in every instance to constitute the food of an infant, unless such an arrangement is impracticable. After the child is weaned, fresh cow's milk in which a small portion of soft water has been mingled, and sometimes a little sugar, with a small quantity of crust of bread softened, is usually the most healthy food; but this should be varied by occasional meals of gruel, arrow-root, or sago, and if the child is delicate and shows signs of acidity or flatulence, then a preparation of weak chicken broth or beef tea, freed from fat, and thickened with soft boiled rice, may be given.

The same kind of food ought to be continued, with the addition of good bread (and potatoes, when well cooked, seem as healthy food nearly as bread), till the appearance of the "eye teeth"; when they are fairly through, a portion of soft-boiled egg, and occasionally a little meat, the lean part, well cooked and not highly seasoned, may be given.

continued on next page

For older children with teeth, Hale wrote:

Ripe fruits should never be given to children till they have teeth, and unripe fruits ought never to be eaten.

During childhood and early youth, the breakfast and supper should consist principally of bread and milk, ripe fruits and vegetable food; it will be sufficient to allow a portion of animal food with the dinner.

Fish, chicken, and other white meats are best for children. Fat pork is nearly indigestible for the young and delicate, and ought never to be eaten by them.

Hale called for people to drink water as a safe beverage for all ages. A cup of warm tea was considered good for the stomach. It was advised for people to sip their water and not drink rapidly. Adults were encouraged not to drink cold water when they felt overheated or fatigued. It was believed to be bad for the digestive system and not a good source of quenching one's thirst. Water at room temperature, or warm tea was best in those conditions.

Children were instructed to drink more water and liquids than adults, but a habit of continual drinking was believed to weaken the stomach and render children irritable and peevish. During the cold months, children were encouraged to drink milk instead of their usual water. Mrs. Hale wrote, "Children should take milk—as a substitute, during the winter, good gruel with bread, or water, sweetened with molasses, is healthy. Never give children tea, coffee, or chocolate with their meals."

Indiana

Chicago •

Fort Wayne •

• Peoria

Indianapolis •

• Springfield
• Decatur

Little Pigeon Creek
Community

• Louisville • Lexington

Evansville •

Elizabethtown
• Lincoln Boyhood Home
• Lincoln Birthplace

• Bowling Green

*E*ighteen-sixteen was known as "the year without a summer." Even in July, frost killed the crops and gardens of Kentucky families. In November of that year, Thomas Lincoln went to Indiana to purchase property. Land sold for less than three dollars per acre, and Thomas Lincoln purchased eighty acres in Hurricane Township of what was then Perry County. He marked his property by placing huge piles of brush on each corner. He then constructed a half-faced cabin which his family would use as shelter for a few days while waiting for their cabin to be built.

In December 1816 the Lincoln family began the five-day journey to their new home. This time they traveled ninety-one miles, and crossed the Ohio River by ferry to Bates Landing. From there, it was another sixteen miles to the homestead. Lincoln wrote, "We reached our new home about the time the State came into Union." According to Lincoln, Indiana was "a wild region, with many bears and other wild animals still in the woods." At night, they could hear the panthers scream. Here the family settled into a heavily wooded area which had to be cleared for crops, a home, a barn, and a garden. As Lincoln himself said, "Here I grew up."

It was in Indiana that Lincoln grew from a boy of seven years of age to a man. It was also in Indiana that Lincoln became acquainted with death and the profound grief and sorrow that accompanied it. Here, he buried his mother, his sister, and his sister's newborn baby boy.

Lincoln was young, but large for his age, when his family became the twenty-eighth one to move into the Little Pigeon Creek Community. He worked from dawn to dusk helping his family establish their farm. The Lincolns kept chickens, hogs, oxen, a cow, horses, and sheep. Almost immediately, after moving to Indiana, an

continued on next page

ax was put into young Abraham's hands. It was a useful tool in the wilderness, and for the next fourteen years, the young man was seldom without it.

The corn on the Lincolns' Indiana farm grew to amazing heights. A little over a mile from the their home was Noah Gordon's "horse mill," where young Abraham would take shelled corn to be ground into cornmeal—a staple in the pioneer family's diet. Other staples included pork, sorghum, vegetables from mother Nancy's garden, and fruit from the small orchard.

Rail Splitters

1	egg
3	tablespoons sugar
1	teaspoon salt
1	cup yellow corn meal
4	tablespoons melted lard, shortening, or butter
1	cup fresh buttermilk
½	teaspoon baking soda
1	teaspoon cold water
1	cup flour
4	teaspoons baking powder

Grease and flour a corn-muffin pan. Preheat over to 375 degrees.

Melt lard, shortening, or butter, and let cool a bit (it should not be hot.). Mix sugar, salt, and corn meal. Add beaten egg. Mix well. Slowly add melted fat. Mix again. Add buttermilk. Dissolve the baking soda in the 1 teaspoon of cold water. Add to mixture.

Sift flour and 4 teaspoons of baking powder together. Sift into batter.

Pour mixture into prepared muffin pan and bake about 15 minutes, or until golden brown.

When Thomas Lincoln moved to Indiana, he worked as a cask maker for Reuben Grigsby. Reuben made a favorite holiday beverage—applejack brandy. Apples were a favorite among the pioneer families because they could be stored for a lengthy period of time, and because they were versatile. The oldest cookbooks and household books include recipes and instructions for drying apples for winter. Applesauce and apple butter were both made in large iron kettles, and usually cooked outdoors. It was recommended that applesauce be eaten with pork during the winter months as part of a healthy diet. Apples were stewed, baked, fried, sauced, and juiced. They were used in pies, tarts, dumplings, cobblers, and jellies. However, to most children, including the Lincoln children, a ripe apple fresh from the tree was a tasty treat. The green apples that the Lincolns enjoyed fried were the green or transparent apples which ripen in June. Granny Smith apples also are a suitable choice for frying. One should never use unripe fruit for cooking or eating at any time.

Fried Green Apples

2	tablespoons butter
1	cup sugar
	Cinnamon
3	to 4 green apples (peeled or unpeeled), sliced

Melt butter in a skillet over medium heat. (Note: If cooking over a fire, keep skillet near but not directlly over the flames. A few coals under a spider skillet are acceptable.) Drop in sliced green apples; sprinkle with sugar and cinnamon to taste. Cook slowly, stirring occasionally until apples are browned and tender.

Both the purplish roots and the green leaves of beets are edible, and both are high in vitamin C. It has been said that Lincoln "knew and tolerated" beets. Beets prepared in this method can be either refrigerated until ready to use, or sealed in sterilized jars in a 10-minute boiling water bath.

Sweet Pickled Beets

Young beets
Boiling water
Sugar
Vinegar
Whole cloves

Peel small beets in a porcelain or enamel saucepan and add boiling water. Cook until beets are tender; set aside until cool.

Boil equal parts of sugar and vinegar along with ½ teaspoon cloves for every gallon of liquid used. Cloves should be tied in a cheesecloth bag. Pour sugar liquid over the beets. Allow to set until ready to use.

The Lincolns brought a few hogs and one cow when they moved to Indiana from Kentucky. Every fall, a hog was butchered to be used for the family's meat during the winter. Pork was a staple in Lincoln's diet.

Nancy's Pork Chops and Greens

6   thick pork chops
1   large clove garlic, minced
1   bay leaf
    Bit of flour
¼   cup water
¼   cup vinegar
    Salt and pepper
    Green vegetables of
        choice (such as
        cabbage, spinach, or
        green beans)

Season and flour pork chops. Brown them in hot fat. Add rest of ingredients and simmer until tender. Add more water if necessary. After meat is done, add green vegetables and cook in the liquid until tender.

Leaveners

In the 1790s, bakers found a way to make dough rise effectively. Potassium carbonate, commonly called pearlash, was widely used until the introduction of baking soda in 1840. Baking soda, or saleratus, was more effective, but required the addition of sour milk or cream of tartar to make dough rise sufficiently. This problem was solved in 1856 when baking soda and cream of tartar were combined and sold commercially. The new product was named baking powder, and with its introduction on the market, cooks saved hours of beating eggs and batter. Yeast, the most effective dough rising product, became commercially available sometimes around 1868. There were recipes for homemade yeast prior to this date, and it was indeed frequently made at home. Without a doubt, the commercial production of yeast made life a bit easier for the post-Civil War baker.

Gingerbread

Lincoln often told this story involving gingerbread men:

Once in a while my mother used to get some sorghum and some ginger and mix us up a batch of gingerbread. It wasn't often, and it was our biggest treat. One day I smelled it and came into the house to get my share while it was hot. I found she had baked me three gingerbread men, and I took them out under a hickory tree to eat them.

There was a family near us that was a little poorer than we were, and their boy came along as I sat down.

"Abe," he said, edging close, "gimme a man."

I gave him one. He crammed it into his mouth at two bites and looked at me while I bit the legs from my first one.

"Abe," he said, "gimme that other'n."

I wanted it, but I gave it to him, and as it followed the first one I said, "You seem to like gingerbread."

"Abe," he said earnestly, "I don't s'pose there's anybody on this earth likes gingerbread as well as I do,"— and drawing a sigh that brought up crumbs — "an' I don't s'pose there's anybody gets less of it."

Young Abe's Gingerbread Men

1	cup butter
½	cup dark molasses or sorghum
1	cup sugar
1	teaspoon cinnamon
1	teaspoon ginger
1	teaspoon nutmeg
1	teaspoon cloves
2	eggs, well beaten
1	teaspoon vinegar
5	cups flour
1	teaspoon baking soda

Cream butter and sugar together. Add molasses, cinnamon, nutmeg, ginger, and cloves. Mix well. Pour into a saucepan. Bring to a boil, stirring constantly. As the mixture reaches the boiling point, remove from heat. Cool to lukewarm. Add eggs and vinegar; mix well. Sift together flour and baking soda; add to egg mixture. Mix again until mixture forms a smooth dough. Cover or wrap dough and place in a cool place (or in a refrigerator) for several hours or overnight.

When ready to bake, roll out on floured board. Cut with gingerbread-man cutter or other desired shape. Raisins or other pieces of dried fruit can be used to decorate. Bake in preheated 350 degree oven on an ungreased cookie sheet for 8–10 minutes for four-inch cookies, or 6–7 minutes for one-inch cookies.

If preferred, cookies can be decorated with frosting after they have cooled.

Just as Lincoln enjoyed sorghum, so will anyone who tries this cake-like gingerbread.

Hot Water Sorghum Gingerbread

⅓ cup shortening
⅔ cup boiling water
1 cup sorghum
1 egg, well beaten
2 ¾ cups flour
2 teaspoons baking soda
1 teaspoon salt
1 ½ teaspoons ground ginger
1 teaspoon cinnamon
¼ teaspoon cloves

Grease and flour a 9 x 9-inch baking pan. Preheat oven to 350 degrees.

Melt shortening in boiling water. Remove from heat and let cool a bit. (If water is too hot, the egg will cook instead of blend.) Add sorghum and beaten egg. Sift dry ingredients together. Add to sorghum mixture and mix thoroughly. Pour batter into prepared pan and bake for 30 minutes.

Serve with whipped cream or ice cream.

For decades, this recipe was common throughout the United States before Sarah Hale published it in 1841.

Common Gingerbread

(historic version)

Take a pound and a half of flour, and rub into it half a pound of butter; add half a pound of brown sugar and half a pint of molasses, two table-spoonfuls of cream, a teaspoonful of pearlash, and ginger to the taste. Make it into a stiff paste, and roll it out thin. Put it on buttered tins, and bake in a moderate oven.

Above: A replica of the Lincoln cabin in Little Pigeon Creek Community in Southern Indiana. (Courtesy of Lincoln Pioneer Village and Museum, Rockport, Indiana.)

Left: A fireplace and hearth similar to the ones used when Lincoln was a boy. Note the Dutch ovens on the hearth.

Sweeteners

In pioneer America, sugar was not always readily available. Many homes contained sugar chests which could be locked, and the lady of the house, or a trusted servant, kept the key on her person. At times, sugar sold for as much as five dollars per pound. For cooks such as Nancy Lincoln, and later Sally Lincoln, alternatives were a necessity.

Molasses is a thick, rich, syrup separated from raw sugar during the refining process. There are four types of molasses, and all are high in calcium and iron. Light molasses has the mildest taste; dark molasses is heavier and less sweet; blackstrap molasses is a bitter waste product of sugar manufacturing; unsulphured molasses contains no sulphur dioxide and is specially manufactured from the juice of sun-ripened sugar cane.

Maple syrup is made from the sweet thick sap of maple trees.

Honey is a sweet, thick syrup made by honey bees. It is a nutritious sweetener which aides in the digestion process and contains iron, riboflavin, and vitamin C. Generally, the lighter the honey in color, the more flavorful it is. Darker honey tends to have a stronger taste and should not be used in baking. When honey is used in cakes and breads, their keeping quality is enhanced. By using a slightly higher temperature, honey can be substituted for sugar in jams, jellies, and candies. To substitute honey used the following guidelines:

For breads, rolls, and general cooking, 1 cup of honey equals 1 cup of sugar.

For cakes and cookies, ⅞ cup of honey equals 1 cup of sugar.

In all other recipes, reduce any other liquid specified in a recipe by 3 tablespoons for each cup of honey substituted.

continued next page

Sorghum is a dark syrup made from the sweet juices of the sorghum plant. It can be used in recipes which would normally call for molasses, but do not use it in jams or jellies. Sorghum has a unique flavor of its own, and it is also a wonderful condiment on fresh-baked breads and biscuits.

Honey and Almond Cake

½	cup shortening
½	teaspoon salt
½	teaspoon ginger
½	teaspoon cinnamon
1 ¼	cups honey
2	eggs
1	cup blanched, chopped almonds
2 ½	cups sifted cake flour
¼	teaspoon baking soda
1	teaspoon baking powder
½	cup water

Preheat oven to 325 degrees. Grease and flour a 9 x 9-inch baking pan.

Cream together shortening, salt, ginger, and cinnamon. Add 1 cup of the honey and mix till well blended. Beat in eggs one at a time.

Combine cake flour, baking soda, and baking powder; add to shortening and honey mixture alternately with water, blending well but not overbeating. Pour into prepared baking pan. Mix remaining honey with almonds and sprinkle over the top of the batter. (Do not pile them too high in one spot, they will cause the cake to collapse.) Bake for 60 minutes, or until cake tests done.

(Note: To blanch almonds, drop them in boiling water for a few seconds, then plunge them into cold water. The brown skins will then slip off easily. Almonds are easier to chop while they are still slightly damp.)

Milk sickness came to Indiana in the fall of 1818. This fatal disease was caused by an innocent-looking white wildflower commonly called snakeroot. As other vegetation died in the sweltering heat during a humid summer, snakeroot flourished. The cows would eat it, become sick, tremble, and die. People who drank milk from an infected cow were likely to take to their beds, fall into a coma, and die also.

Many members of the Little Pigeon Creek Community fell victim to this illness. Nancy Lincoln's Uncle Tom Sparrow and his wife Elizabeth both died leaving their nephew, Dennis Hanks, to live with the Lincoln family. Nancy helped tend her sick relatives. Thomas Lincoln made the coffins, and young Abraham made the pegs which held the coffins together. On October 5, 1818, Nancy fell victim to milk sickness and succumbed. Her husband made her coffin, and her son whittled the pegs. She was buried on a knoll a quarter of a mile from the Lincoln cabin, and near the graves of her uncle and aunt.

In late November of the following year, Thomas Lincoln traveled to Elizabethtown, Kentucky. There, on December 2, he married Sally Bush Johnston, a widow with three children. The Lincoln cabin became crowded as there were now eight people living in it: Thomas, his new wife, his children Sarah and Abraham, Dennis Hanks, and Sally's three children: Elizabeth, John D., and Matilda. Sally brought a few belongings with her, including a bureau, a table, a clothespress, bedclothes, and kitchenware. But what Abraham was most interested in were the four books Sally brought—*Webster's Speller*, *Robinson Crusoe*, *The Arabian Nights*, and *Lessons in Elocution* by William Scott.

This cooked cornmeal mixture is also known as mush.

Sally Johnston's Hasty Pudding

4   cups water
1   cup yellow or white
      cornmeal
1   teaspoon salt

Bring three cups of water to a boil in a saucepan.

Mix cornmeal and salt with the remaining 1 cup of cold water. Mix well. Slowly pour the mixture into the boiling water, stirring all the while. Cook until thickened, stirring often. Cover and continue to cook over very low heat for another 10 minutes. Serve hot.

Left-over pudding can be poured into a baking dish and stored in the refrigerator. It can then be sliced and fried in bacon drippings and eaten crisp.

> *Abraham Lincoln is my nam[e]*
>   *And with my pen I wrote the same[.]*
> *I wrote in both hast[e] and speed*
>   *and left it here for fools to read.*
> *Abraham Lincoln*

For special dinners, feast, or celebrations, women would gather edible flower petals and leaves such as those from roses, pansies, borage, and wild mint. These were then used in teas, or candied to be used as an edible decoration for other foods.

Candied Mint Leaves

Fresh mint leaves or flower
    petals
Egg whites
Sugar (powdered or granulated
    works)

Wash the leaves and petals carefully. Dry on a towel, keeping them unbroken. Dip each one into unbeaten egg whites. Press into the sugar and spread out on a board to dry. Shake off excess sugar. Place in the refrigerator to harden.

Sprinkle in a salad, on top of fruit, on top of a cake, in a punch bowl, or eat like candy.

Abraham Lincoln,
    His hand and pen.
He will be good,
    But God knows when.

On August 4, 1826, Sarah Lincoln married Aaron Grigsby, the eldest son of Reuben Grigsby. To commemorate his sister's wedding, young Abraham wrote a poem which was read at the reception.

As Adam was resting in slumber
He lost a short rib from his side.
And when he awoke 'twas in wonder
to see a most beautiful bride.

The Lord then was not willing
The man should be alone,
But caused a sleep upon him
And took from him a bone.

The woman was not taken
From Adam's feet we see,
So he must not abuse her
The meaning seems to be.

This woman, she was taken
From under Adam's arm.
So she must be protected
From injuries and harm.

Sarah Lincoln's Wedding Dinner

Two fat wild turkeys roasted a rich brown

A saddle of deer meat

Six large vegetable pies, full of turnips, beans, and potatoes

A big bowl of wild honey

A bowl of maple sugar

At least a hundred fried Kentucky Wonders

Watermelon preserves

Cherry preserves

Bushel of pawpaws

Tea

Vegetable Pies

	Pastry for double-crust pie
3	turnips
3	potatoes
2	cups green beans
1	onion
3	carrots
	Other vegetables as desired (celery, corn, okra)
3	tablespoons butter
2	tablespoons flour
2	cups of chicken or turkey broth
1	teaspoon ground rosemary
	Salt and pepper to taste
1	egg, beaten

Cut all vegetables into small chunks and set aside. In a large skillet, heat the butter until it bubbles. Sprinkle over with flour; stir until it forms a smooth paste. Gradually add the two cups of broth. Cook over medium heat, stirring constantly until thick and creamy. Add the cut vegetables and rosemary. Season to taste. Heat thoroughly.

Preheat oven to 350 degrees. Roll out half of the pastry and place it in a greased casserole dish, leaving a 1-inch overhang. Spoon the hot vegetable mixture into the pastry. Roll out remaining pastry and fit over filling. Trim and crimp crusts together. Slash steam vents in a decorative pattern on upper crust. Brush with beaten egg. Bake for 45–60 minutes or until crust is golden brown and vegetables are done.

Kentucky Wonders

3 tablespoons lard or butter
3 eggs
3 tablespoons sugar
   Sifted flour

Melt lard or butter and allow to cool; add eggs and mix well. Add sugar and beat mixture. Add enough sifted flour to make a dough (similar to pie dough).

Roll dough to about ⅛-inch thickness. Cut into squares three inches long and two inches wide. Cut several slits lengthwise to within a quarter of an inch of the edges of the pieces of dough. Run two forefingers through every other slit. Lay them down on the board lengthwise and dent them. Fry in hot lard or oil until a light brown.

This recipe works well for almost any fruit.

Cherry Preserves

Wash the desired amount of cherries. Remove stems and pits. Mash and add honey to taste. If the cherries are very juicy (or if other types of fruit are very juicy) stir in either a little wheat germ or flour; add just enough to thicken the jam as you want it. Tiny new mint leaves may also be shredded up and added for a unique flavor. Keep refrigerated in a covered dish.

Watermelon Preserves

11 cups watermelon rind
9 cups sugar
8 cups water
2 oranges, sliced
4 lemons, sliced
2 sticks cinnamon
4 teaspoons powdered
cloves

Wash watermelon rinds. Peel the outer green skin, leaving the white portion of rind. Cut the rind into one-inch chunks. Place in a large saucepan or kettle with ½ cups salt to one gallon of water and soak for at least eight hours. Drain the salt water. Replace with fresh water and cook rind chunks until tender, about 30 minutes.

In another saucepan combine sugar, the 8 cups of water, orange and lemon slices, cinnamon sticks, and powdered cloves. Boil for five minutes. Add watermelon rind and cook until translucent.

Pour into hot sterilized jars and seal in a boiling water bath for 10 minutes.

On January 20, 1828, Abraham Lincoln's beloved sister, Sarah, died in childbirth. She was buried holding her baby boy in her arms in the Little Pigeon Creek Baptist Church Cemetery.

The Lincoln family left Indiana in the spring of 1830. Abraham thought he might never go back to the Little Pigeon Creek Community again, but he did return years later.

Lincoln described his visit:

In the fall of 1844, thinking I might aid some to carry the State of Indiana for Mr. Clay, I went into the neighborhood in that State in which I was raised, where my mother and only sister were buried, and from which I had been absent about fifteen years. That part of the country is, within itself, as unpoetical as any spot of the earth; but still, seeing it and its objects and inhabitants aroused feelings in me which were certainly poetry; though whether my expression of these feelings is poetry is quite another question.

Upon returning to Indiana, and seeing his old friends and neighbors, Lincoln was inspired to write the following poem:

My Childhood's Home

My childhood's home I see again.
  And sadden with the view;
And still, as memory crowds my brain,
  There's pleasure in it too.

O Memory! thou midway world
  'Twixt earth and paradise,
Where things decayed and loved ones lost
  In dreamy shadows rise,

And, freed from all that's earthly vile,
  Seem hallowed, pure, and bright,
Like scenes in some enchanted isle
  All bathed in liquid light.

As dusky mountains please the eye
  When twilight chases day;
As bugle-notes that, passing by,
  In distance die away;

continued on next page

As leaving some grand waterfall,
　　We, lingering, list its roar —
So memory will hallow all
　　We've known, but know no more.

Near twenty years have passed away
　　Since here I bid farewell
To woods and fields, and scenes of play,
　　And playmates loved so well.

Where many were, but few remain
　　Of old familiar things,
But seeing them, to mind again,
　　The lost and absent brings.

The friends I left the parting day,
　　How changed, as time has sped!
Young childhood grown, strong manhood gray,
　　And half of all are dead.

I hear the loved survivors tell
　　How nought from death could save,
Till every sound appears a knell,
　　And every spot a grave.

I range the field with pensive tread
　　And pace the hollow rooms,
And feel (companion of the dead)
　　I'm living in the tombs.

(*Above*) In eighteenth-century homes such as that of Mary Todd's, kitchens were often separate from the house, to use in the hot summer months to avoid heating up the house—and to reduce risk of fire. The Todds' meals were cooked in the separate kitchen and brought to the warming kitchen in the house (*shown above and left*) and kept warm in the ovens and on the hearth until serving time. Kitchen utensils like those used then are shown displayed in a pie safe in the Todd home (*below*).

The nursery in the Todd home (*above*) held a variety of dolls, toys, and small furnishings to delight the children of the family, and give them a place to play away from the costly and elegant furnishings of the parlor (*right*).

When Abraham Lincoln met his wife's family for the first time at the Todd home in Lexington, the family lined up on the stairs in hierarchical order—Papa, Mama, children, and servants—to meet their new in-law.

The dining room in the Todd home.

This portrait of Mary Todd Lincoln was painted around the turn of the twentieth century by her niece, Katherine Helm, at the request of Robert Todd Lincoln. (Townsend Collection of Mary Genevieve Townsend Murphy)

Illinois

Chicago

Fort Wayne

Peoria

Springfield

Indianapolis

Decatur

Little Pigeon Creek
Community

Louisville   Lexington

Evansville

Elizabethtown

Lincoln Boyhood Home

Lincoln Birthplace

Bowling Green

After saying good-bye at his mother's gravesite, Lincoln and his extended family were ready to leave the Little Pigeon Creek community to settle in Coles County, Illinois. On March 1, 1930, three wagons containing thirteen people pulled out of the area Lincoln had called home for fourteen years. He was then twenty-one years old.

Lincoln stayed with his family for about a year, helping them establish their new home. Then, in July 1831, Lincoln settled in New Salem, Illinois, a small thriving settlement. For a while he lived at the Rutledge Tavern and took most of his meals there. He sharpened his grammar skills and studied to become a lawyer. In New Salem the young man developed his interest in politics, and was twice elected as the district's representative to the state legislative body. He was part of what was knows as "The Long Nine," a group of men known for their height, who were instrumental in moving the Illinois state capital from Vandalia to Springfield.

Soon Lincoln found himself moving to Springfield. When he arrived, he stopped at the store belonging to Joshua Speed and inquired about the price of bedding. Upon realizing that Lincoln did not have enough money to purchase a bed, Joshua said that he had one and that Lincoln could live with him above the store. Beds were a luxury for many, and Lincoln considered himself fortunate to find a place to sleep. He carried his dusty saddlebags upstairs, and upon returning said, "Well, Speed, I am moved."

Lincoln became the junior law partner to John Todd Stuart, and through him became part of Springfield's social scene. Tall and awkward, Lincoln lacked many of the social graces which most women found attractive in a man. Besides that, he was neither a handsome nor a genteel man. But he did posses a quick mind and a keen sense of humor. No one could tell a story better than Abraham Lincoln. It was this quality that first caught the attention of Mary Ann Todd, a Southern belle who was residing in Springfield.

Mary's two older, married sisters, Elizabeth Edwards and Frances

Lincoln's Table

Wallace, both lived in Springfield. Elizabeth had married Ninian Edwards, the son of Illinois' only territorial governor. Frances had married William Wallace, a local pharmacist.

Mary was a five-foot, three-inch, blue-eyed beauty who had received a remarkable education. She had come from Lexington, Kentucky, to stay with her sister Elizabeth, who hoped Mary would find a suitable husband in Springfield. Possessing an infectious laugh and a quick wit, Mary looked intensely at people when they spoke, as if hanging onto their every word. Several men desired to be her dance partner, her escort, and a few desired to be her husband. They found her to be interesting, enthralling, and beautiful. Ninian Edwards once remarked, "Mary could make a bishop forget his prayers."

At a party hosted by Elizabeth, Mary did meet her candidate for the position of "suitable husband." Young Mr. Lincoln knew of this warm, cheery, and vivacious lass through John Todd Stuart, his law partner and Mary's first cousin. After the couple had been introduced, Lincoln boldly held out his hand, bowed slightly, and said, "Miss Todd, I wish to dance with you in the worst way." After a few turns across the dance floor with her awkward dance partner, Mary returned to the other young ladies and assured them that Lincoln had indeed danced in the worst way possible.

Despite that less than perfect first dance, the two began courting. Soon, they discovered their many common interests. They both enjoyed poetry, especially that of Scotland's noble bard, Robert Burns. They shared an interest in theatre, especially the plays of William Shakespeare. Often, the couple could be found in Elizabeth's parlor reading Shakespearean scenes to one another. Politically, they held the same views—they were both Whigs. Women could not yet vote, but that did not stop Mary from having political opinions. She had been raised in a political home where politics permeated the conversation, the entertainment, and the business of the household. Mary's father, Robert Smith Todd, was a supporter and friend to Henry Clay, a frequent guest in the Todd home. Lincoln admired Clay greatly. Lincoln and Mary soon found they had much in common.

To many, including Mary's sister Elizabeth, Lincoln and Mary were mismatched. He was tall and lanky; she was short and slightly round. He had been born and raised in frontier log cabins; she had been born and raised in stately brick mansions. He had lived in the backwoods and wilderness; she had lived in Lexington, Kentucky, the "Athens of the West." He had little schooling; Mary had received twelve years of formal education. Lincoln was in debt; Mary was the daughter of a wealthy businessman.

Despite their differences, the two were drawn together. Against all odds, and against her family's wishes, Mary and Abraham became a couple.

They did have a difficult courtship, and even broke their engagement sometime around the first of January 1841. After months of separation, friends, Mr. and Mrs. Simeon Francis, held a dinner party that brought the two together again. They courted in secret without telling Mary's sister. Finally, they separately told Ninian and Elizabeth that they planned to marry. Elizabeth was livid. The room was filled with words such as "plebeian" and "white trash." Mary, quite the dramatic woman herself, held her ground. She would marry Mr. Lincoln! Eventually, Ninian intervened and made Elizabeth realize the wedding was going to take place and that it would take place in their home. Elizabeth snapped that she did not have time to bake a proper wedding cake, and that she would have to send out for gingerbread and beer. Mary retorted that would be good enough for "plebeians." Invitations were quickly sent to a select few relatives and friends. Frances came to help Elizabeth make preparations. She later commented that she had never worked harder in her life than on Mary's wedding day. The two sisters joined forces, and Mary did have a proper wedding cake—it was still warm when she and Abraham sliced it.

Afterwards, the newlyweds lived in a four-dollar-per-week boarding room at the Globe Tavern. Many have discussed the humbleness of the Lincolns' beginnings at the Globe Tavern. In fact, the Globe Tavern was a respectable, middle-class, boarding house where many young married couples first took up residence, including Mary's sister Frances and her husband William Wallace and cousin John Todd Stuart and his wife.

Lincoln's Table

Soon after the birth of their first son, Robert, the Lincolns moved to a rented cottage and then purchased a house on the corner of Eighth and Jackson streets. There, where they lived for the next seventeen years, the family grew as three more boys were born. Mary was a doting mother; Lincoln was a permissive father. In an era when children's birthdays were seldom celebrated, Mary held birthday parties for her sons, sometimes inviting as many as fifty other children.

Much has been said about the Lincoln marriage. Mary was quick-tempered, feisty, and given to emotional mood swings. Abraham was sometimes melancholy, a workaholic, and sometimes absent from the home for months at a time. They were truly opposites in many ways. Separately, they were both highly sensitive and emotionally unstable. But together they shared a deep, profound love that only the two of them completely understood. He was her "Mr. Lincoln" and she was his "Molly."

Abraham Lincoln in 1860.
(Courtesy Abe's Antiques of Gettysburg)

Mary Todd Lincoln about 1846.
(Donna McCreary collection)

Mary Lincoln wrote home to her Kentucky family asking for a beaten biscuit recipe. This old recipe appears as Mary would have used it.

Beaten Biscuits

(historical version)

One quart of flour, lard the size of a hen's egg, one teaspoonful of salt. Make into a moderately stiff dough with sweet milk. Beat for half an hour. Make out with the hand or cut with the biscuit cutter. Stick with a fork and bake in a hot oven, yet not sufficiently hot to blister the biscuit.

Beaten Biscuits

(modern version)

8	cups sifted flour
¼	teaspoon soda
½	teaspoon sugar
¾	cup lard
1	teaspoon salt
1	cup water

Sift flour, salt, and soda together. Cut in lard until the consistency of fine meal. Stir in 1 cup water; blend thoroughly. Place dough on a wooden block; pound with a hammer, turning frequently, for 20–30 minutes or until dough blisters and becomes satiny in texture.

Roll dough to ½-inch thickness; cut with a small biscuit cutter. Bake in preheated oven at 400 degrees for 25 minutes or until lightly browned.

Fricasseed Chicken

2	to 3 fryers, cut up
	Salt and pepper to taste
	Flour for dredging
	Lard or shortening
½	pint cream
¼	teaspoon nutmeg
¼	teaspoon mace
1	small piece of butter, rolled in a little flour
	Parsley sprigs

Cut chickens into pieces. Wipe pieces dry, season with salt and pepper, and dredge lightly with flour. Melt lard or shortening in frying pan, add chicken and fry until brown on all sides. When done, transfer to a covered pan and keep warm.

Skim the drippings in the frying pan, and add the cream. Season with nutmeg, mace, salt, and pepper. Thicken gravy with the small bit of butter rolled in flour. Stir carefully to be sure that the mixture is smooth. Bring to a good boil, then pour it over the hot chicken. Add a little more lard or butter into the frying pan. Fry the parsley sprigs but keep it green and crisp. Garnish the chicken with parsley.

❧

According to Isaac Arnold, a grand feast was held while he visited the Lincolns. Venison, wild turkey, prairie chickens, quail, and other game were served.

White Fricassee of Chicken

2   to 3 fryers, cut up
      Salt and pepper to taste
¼   teaspoon nutmeg
¼   teaspoon mace
      Sweet marjoram
½   pint cream
      A bit of butter rolled in
         flour
      Small forcemeat balls*
         (optional)

Cut chickens into desired pieces and remove skin. Season with salt, pepper, nutmeg, and mace. Sprinkle some shredded marjoram over the chicken. Put all into a stew pot, and pour in the cream or whole milk. Add butter rolled in flour, and if you choose, the forcemeat balls. Set the stew pan over a low flame. Keep it tightly covered, and stew or simmer gently until the chicken is quite tender, but do not allow to boil. Serve hot.

(* *Forcemeat is finely chopped, highly seasoned meat mixed with bread crumbs, similar to sausage.*)

Broiled Beefsteak

¾   pound of meat and bone
         per person
      Salt and pepper
      Butter
      English mustard

Trim excess fat from meat. Rinse and wipe the steak dry. Place in a broiling pan and place three inches from the heat source in a hot broiling rack. When steak becomes browned, turn with two spoons to prevent piercing the meat. Broil for 10 more minutes for rare meat, longer for well done meat. Place steak on a hot platter. Season with salt and pepper. Dot with butter. Skim off the fat from the drippings and pour the juice over the meat. Serve hot with English mustard.

Butter-Browned Steak with Coffee-Mustard Sauce

4   club, shell, or strip steaks
      cut 1-inch thick
2   tablespoons butter
      Salt and pepper to season
4   teaspoons spicy prepared
      mustard
⅔   cup strong hot coffee

In a very large, heavy, skillet, melt butter. Place steaks in skillet and brown quickly on both sides. For a rare steak, remove to a hot platter and keep warm. For a medium-rare or medium steak, turn the heat under the skillet to low and let the steaks cook slowly for 5–8 minutes longer. (Cook longer for a well-done steak.)

Remove steaks to a platter. Sprinkle steaks with salt and pepper. Spread 1 teaspoon of mustard on each steak. Pour coffee into the skillet and quickly bring to a simmer, scraping up the browned bits on the bottom of the skillet. Pour over steaks and serve.

Mary paid eighty-seven cents at Irwin's Store for a copy of *Miss Leslie's House Book or Manual of Domestic Economy for Town and Country.*

Oysters

In ninteenth-century America, oysters were enormous, commonly six to eight inches in diameter. These special treats were consumed in great quantities and celebrated with oyster parties. Many Americans, including the Lincolns, hosted oyster feasts where oysters were served exclusively and in every conceivable manner. At one of these soirees guests would likely dine on oysters that were boiled, broiled, deviled, curried, fricasseed, panned, scalloped, pickled, stewed, or steamed. The shellfish were also used in pies, omelets, catsups, and fritters.

Scalloped Oysters

(Note: Never have more than a double layer of oysters in this dish. The middle will not bake.)

1   pint of oysters
2   tablespoons light cream
½   cup day-old bread crumbs
1   cup cracker crumbs
½   cup melted butter
Salt and freshly ground pepper
Paprika

Preheat oven to 425 degrees. Drain oysters, reserving ¼ cup of the liquid Combine oyster liquid and cream; set aside. Mix both kinds of crumbs together; add melted butter. Sprinkle a thick layer of crumbs in a 1-quart casserole dish. Cover with half of the oysters, followed by half of the cream mixture. Sprinkle lightly with salt and pepper. Cover with the second layer of crumbs, then oysters, then cream. Add more salt and pepper. Cover with remaining crumbs. Sprinkle with paprika. Bake for 30 minutes.

Steamed Oysters

1   quart of oysters
     Salt and pepper to taste
     Butter

Drain oysters and place in a shallow baking dish or small cake pan. Put the pan into a steamer over boiling water. Steam the oysters until they become plump with curled edges. Do not overcook. Transfer the oysters to a heated serving dish. Dot with butter. Season with salt and pepper to taste. Serve immediately.

Steamed Oysters in the Shell

Wash and scrub the oysters and place them in a pan or casserole with tight-fitting lid. The upper shells must be facing downward to prevent the oyster liquor from running out when the shells open.

Place the pan or casserole over a kettle of rapidly boiling water and steam until the shells open, about 10 minutes.

Oyster Pie

1	tablespoon butter
2	onions, chopped
1	rib celery, chopped
3	tablespoon butter
3	tablespoons flour
1	cup milk
½	cup of oyster liquor
	Dash of mace
	Dash of thyme
	Pinch of minced parsley
1	pint of oysters
	Sherry
	Pastry for 2-crust pie

Melt the 1 tablespoon butter, add the onion and celery and cook until tender. Add the 3 tablespoons of butter and the 3 tablespoons of flour. Mix well. Add milk and oyster liquor. Add spices. Add oysters. Cook until the edges of the oysters curl. Add just enough sherry to thin the sauce. Stir.

Preheat oven to 375 degrees. Pour oyster mixture into a pastry shell and cover with remaining pastry. Bake for 40–50 minutes until browned

Spiced Crabapples

9	pounds crabapples
1	pint vinegar
4	pounds sugar
1	teaspoon whole cloves
3	or 4 cinnamon sticks
	Dash of mace

Peel and cut crabapples in half. Place in a large kettle. Add vinegar, sugar, and spices. Boil for ½ hour, removing before the apples become too soft.

These can be stored in the refrigerator if they will be used in a short period of time. For long term storage, place in sterilized jars and seal by processing in a 10-minutes boiling water bath.

The ladies of New Salem remembered that Lincoln was fond of their fruit pies. After he was elected President, they would bake pies and ship them to him in Washington. Often, they would vent the pie by shaping a letter into the crust for what type of pie it was. An "A" represented an apple pie, "G" was a gooseberry. Sometimes, the pie was vented with the letter "L" for Lincoln.

New Salem Fruit Pies

Pastry for a double-crust 9-inch pie
1 ½ tablespoon flour
1 cup sugar
¼ teaspoon salt
1 quart of fruit of choice (apples, blueberries, gooseberries, or cherries)

Preheat oven to 450 degrees. Line the pie plate with the unbaked pie crust. Place fruit in the pie shell. Mix together sugar, flour, and salt. Mix well and pour into fruit. Cover the top with top pie crust. Crimp edges; make gashes to let the steam escape. Bake for 10 minutes. Reduce temperature to 350 degrees and bake for another 25–30 minutes.

(Note: If the fruit is tart, such as sour cherries, the sugar content may need to be increased slightly; if the fruit is extremely juicy, such as blackberries, the sugar content may need to be lessened slightly.)

When Lincoln lived in New Salem, Illinois, he was known to eat many of his meals at the Rutledge Tavern. This pie was a favorite.

Rutledge Tavern Squash Pie

1	unbaked 9-inch pie shell
1	egg, separated
2	whole eggs
2	cups milk
2	cups cooked mashed squash
½	teaspoon salt
¼	cup brown sugar
1	tablespoon melted butter
1	teaspoon cinnamon
¼	teaspoon nutmeg
¼	teaspoon ginger

Preheat oven to 450 degrees. Lightly beat the egg white and brush the crust lightly with it. Beat the 2 whole eggs and the 1 egg yolk with milk and squash. Add salt, brown sugar, butter, and spices. Mix together thoroughly.

Pour mixture into prepared pie shell. Bake for 10 minutes; reduce heat to 300 degrees and bake for 40–50 minutes, or until set.

Two views of the Lincoln
home in Springfield, Illinois.

Lincoln Home National Historic Site, Springfield, Illinois

Donna McCreary Collection

The stove shown at right, a cast-iron Royal
Oak Number 9, is the second stove the
Lincolns purchased. Manufactured by Jewett
and Root of Buffalo, New York, the stove is a
woodburner with four lids and a wide hearth.
It was used by the family prior to their
departure for Washington, and is still in good,
serviceable condition.

The stove was purchased from dealer Eli
Kreigh in Springfield on June 9, 1860, just
after the primary elections. Because they
would be entertaining more, Mary decided
they needed a better and larger stove than the
one she had, thus precipitating the purchase
of this one. She would have liked to have
taken it to the White House, but realized that
she would not be doing the cooking once they
got there. (Lincoln Home National Historic
Site, Springfield, Illinois)

In 1841, Lincoln traveled to Louisville, Kentucky to visit his friend Joshua Speed at his family's home, Farmington. Miss Mary Speed was Joshua's older sister. She was forty-one years old at the time of Lincoln's visit.

After returning to Springfield, Lincoln wrote to her saying, "I am literally subsisting on savory remembrances—that is, being unable to eat, I am living upon the remembrance of the delicious dishes of peaches and cream we used to have at your house."

Miss Mary Speed's Peach Pie

Pastry for double crust 9-inch pie
2 cups peeled, sliced peaches
⅓ cup sugar
1 teaspoon lemon juice
2 teaspoon butter
⅓ cups sugar

Preheat oven to 425 degrees. Line a 9-inch pie pan with half of pastry and sprinkle it lightly with ⅓ cup of sugar.

Place peaches in pastry. Pour lemon juice evenly over the peaches. Dot with butter. Sprinkle rest of sugar over the top of the peaches. Cover with remaining pastry. Crimp edges and cut vents in the top of the pastry to permit steam to escape. Brush the pastry top with cream or melted butter. Bake for 10 minutes. Reduce oven temperature to 350 degrees and bake for 35–40 minutes.

Serve warm with whipped cream or vanilla ice cream.

Lincoln's Fruit Cookies

1 ½ cups sugar
1 cup soft butter
1 slightly beaten egg
1 teaspoon grated nutmeg
3 tablespoons dried
  currants or raisins
1 teaspoon baking powder
3 ½ cups flour, approximately
3 tablespoons milk
  (approximately)

Preheat oven to 375 degrees. Cream together butter and sugar. Add slightly beaten egg. Add baking powder and nutmeg. Slowly add just enough flour to make the dough rollable. Add dried fruit. Roll the dough smooth. Cut with a large round cookie cutter and place on well-greased cookie sheet. Moisten the top of each cookie with a little milk. Sprinkle with sugar. Bake for 8–10 minutes. (Be careful not to overbake.) Cool on wire rack or on brown paper.

Sangamon County Sour Cream Cookies

2 eggs
2 cups sifted flour
1 cup sugar
½ teaspoon baking soda
¾ cup sour cream

Beat eggs well. Add sugar and sour cream. Mix together thoroughly. Add sifted flour and baking soda. Beat together. Drop by spoonfuls 1 inch apart on a greased cookie sheet. Bake at 350 degrees for 7–10 minutes, or until a light golden brown. Do not overbake.

Variation: Add ¼ teaspoon cinnamon or cloves to the cookie dough.

Mary Todd's Courting Cake
(or Burnt Sugar Cake)

1 ½	cups sugar	1 ½	cups cake flour
½	cup hot water	2	teaspoons baking powder
3	egg whites		Dash of salt
½	cup butter	1	teaspoon vanilla

Preheat oven to 350 degrees. Grease and flour two 8-inch cake pans.

Place ½ cup of sugar in a heavy iron skillet. Heat slowly, stirring continuously with a wooden spoon until the sugar becomes a very dark brown. Add hot water and stir until the sugar dissolves and becomes a caramelized sugar syrup.

Beat egg whites, adding ½ cup of sugar a little at a time, until stiff peaks form. Set aside.

In another bowl, cream butter with remaining ½ cup sugar. Sift together cake flour, baking powder, and salt. Alternately add the flour mixture and the caramelized sugar syrup to the butter-sugar mixture. Fold in the beaten egg whites. Add vanilla. Bake for 45 minutes or until done. Finish cake with frosting (recipe follows).

Frosting for Courting Cake

½	cup butter
1	cup dark brown sugar
⅓	cup milk
2	cups powdered sugar

Melt the butter in a heavy saucepan. Add the dark brown sugar and cook over low heat for 2–3 minutes. Stir constantly. Remove from heat. Add milk, and bring to a boil. Cool to lukewarm warm and gradually stir in powdered sugar. Beat vigorously until mixture is smooth.

*M*onsieur Giron was a short, stout Frenchman who owned a confectionery store on Mill Street in Lexington, Kentucky. His home was a two-story brick building with an iron grill across the balcony of the upper story. According to Mary Todd's sister, Elizabeth, a note was taken to Monsieur Giron to place the bakery order. Elizabeth and Mary both begged to be the courier so they could "feast our eyes on the iced cakes decorated with garlands of pink sugar roses or the bride's spun sugar, pyramiding in the center, veiling tiny fat cupids, or little sugar brides."

It is possible that Monsieur Giron was the creator of the wedding cake for Elizabeth's marriage to Ninian Edwards. He definitely created a cake in honor of the Marquis de Lafayette's visit to Lexington in 1825. The Todd family procured the recipe from Monsieur Giron, and Mary prepared it for Abraham Lincoln. She served it in their home in Springfield, and it was prepared in the White House. Lincoln said it was "the best cake I ever ate." And now, the recipe carries many names: Mary Todd's White Cake, Mary Todd's Vanilla Almond Cake, Mary's Christmas Cake, and Mary Todd Lincoln's White Almond Cake. A versatile cake, which can be enjoyed on many different occasions, it may be prepared in several ways.

Lincoln Home National Historic Site, Springfield, Illinois

The Lincoln family used a lovely Chelsea china pattern in their Springfield home. Broken pieces were found during the extensive renovation of the home. A set of china with the same pattern is on display in the Lincoln Home's dining room(seen at right), although it did not belong to the Lincolns.

Donna McCreary Collection

Mary Todd's White Cake

1 cup chopped blanched almonds
1 cup butter
6 egg whites
2 cups sugar
3 cups sifted flour
1 teaspoon vanilla or almond extract
1 cup milk
3 teaspoons baking powder

Preheat oven to 350 degrees. Grease and flour a bundt or tube cake pan or two 9-inch cake pans. (An old-fashioned fluted copper pan with a center funnel was probably used by Mary Lincoln.)

Grate almonds until they are almost a fine, floury texture. Set aside. Cream butter and sugar; sift flour and baking powder together three times. Add to butter and sugar, alternating with milk. Stir in almonds and beat well.

Beat egg whites until stiff and fold into the cake batter; add vanilla or almond extract. Pour batter into prepared cake pan. Bake for 1 hour or until cake tests done. Turn out on a wire rack and cool.

Frost cake with old-fashioned boiled white icing (recipe follows), or a white cream cheese icing, sprinkle powdered sugar on top, or top with a light glaze. Serve with fresh fruit.

Frosting for Mary Todd's White Cake

2   cups sugar

1   cup water

2   egg whites, stiffly beaten with a few grains of salt

½   cup diced candied pineapple

½   cup crystallized cherries, cut in half

1   teaspoon of vanilla

Boil the sugar and water until the syrup spins a five-inch thread. Slowly fold 4 tablespoons of syrup into the well-beaten egg whites a tablespoon at a time, then add the remaining syrup by slowly pouring it in a thin stream. Beat hard until all is used and the mixture stands in peaks when dropped from a spoon. Add vanilla. Fold in pineapple and cherries.

(Note: If this mixture is not boiled long enough, it will resemble marshmallow cream.)

Variation: Omit the pineapple and cherries. Ice cake and sprinkle grated coconut all over the cake. This was known as Merry Christmas Cake.

Southern Lemon Cake

CAKE:

¾   cup butter

1 ½   cups sugar

4   eggs, separated

1   teaspoon lemon extract

1 ½   cups flour

1 ½   teaspoons baking powder

1   teaspoon salt

¾   cup milk

FILLING:

1   cup sugar

3   tablespoons corn starch

1   cup boiling water

2   eggs

    Juice of 2 large lemons

2   tablespoons butter

FOR CAKE: Grease and flour two 9-inch cake pans. Preheat oven to 350 degrees.

Cream together butter and sugar. Beat egg yolks and add to mixture. Add lemon extract.

Sift together dry ingredients. Alternately add dry ingredients and milk to cream mixture. Beat egg whites until stiff. Fold into batter. Pour into prepared cake pans and bake for 25 minutes. Remove from cake pans and let cool.

FOR FILLING: Mix sugar and corn starch together. Gradually add boiling water. Beat eggs well and add to sugar mixture. Add lemon juice and butter. Cook, stirring constantly until it thickens, about five minutes. Spread on one cooled cake layer and top with remaining cake layer.

If desired, spread butter frosting (recipe follows) on the top and the sides of the cake.

Butter Frosting

1	egg white
1	cup granulated sugar
1	cup warm milk
½	cup shortening
½	cup butter
1	teaspoon vanilla

Beat egg white until very stiff. Add sugar slowly. Add milk slowly. Put aside. Beat remaining ingredients well. Add egg mixture a little at a time, beating well after each addition. It will resemble whipped cream when done.

Election Cake

1	cup currants
½	cup brandy
1	tablespoon sugar
¾	cup scalded milk
1	cake yeast
¼	cup warm water
1	cup unsifted flour
½	cup butter
1	cup sugar
2 ¼	cups sifted flour
½	teaspoon salt
¾	teaspoon mace
1	teaspoon cinnamon
1	egg
1	teaspoon grated lemon rind
2	teaspoons lemon juice

Soak currants overnight in brandy, in a tightly closed container.

Add the 1 tablespoon sugar to the scalded milk; let cool. Crumble yeast into warm water and let dissolve; add to milk. Add the unsifted flour and mix until well blended. Let rise in a warm place until it has doubled in bulk, about 1 hour.

Cream butter and sugar until very light. Add egg and beat until light. Stir in lemon rind and lemon juice. Add yeast mixture and beat thoroughly. Drain the currants and add (reserve the brandy). Sifted flour, salt, mace, and cinnamon together. Add dry ingredients and reserved brandy and mix well. Pour into a well-greased tube pan or a 9 x 5-inch loaf pan. Cover with a cloth and place in a warm place away from a draft. Allow to rise until double in bulk. (This rises very slowly and may take 4 to 6 hours to double in bulk.)

Bake in preheated 375 degree oven for about 45 minutes. Cool in pan briefly. Turn out on a rack and cool further. Brush with Lemon or Orange Glaze (recipe follows).

Lemon or Orange Glaze

1	cup confectioners' sugar
¼	cup lemon or orange juice

Combine sugar and juice. Blend well. Spread thinly over top of cake, allowing the glaze to drizzle down the sides.

Lemon Custard Pie

⅔   cup water
1   cup sugar
4   eggs, separated
1   lemon
1   tablespoon corn starch
3   tablespoons of sugar
    Unbaked 9-inch pie shell

Preheat oven to 325 degrees. Juice the lemon and grate the rind. Combine water, 1 cup sugar, egg yolks, lemon juice and rind, and corn starch. Beat hard for one minute. Pour mixture into pie shell and bake for 30 minutes.

Beat the egg whites, gradually adding the 3 tablespoons of sugar, until very stiff. Place on custard pie. Increase oven heat to 450 degrees; return pie to oven and bake until meringue peaks brown lightly.

Abraham Lincoln enjoyed this lemon pie while staying at a small hotel in Illinois operated by Mrs. Nancy Breedlove.

Meringue-Topped Tart Lemon Custard Pie

CRUST:

1 cup sifted all-purpose flour

¾ teaspoon salt

¼ cup lard

3 to 4 tablespoons cold water

TART LEMON CUSTARD FILLING:

1 cup sugar

1 tablespoon cornstarch

Pinch of salt

Finely grated rind of one large lemon

Juice from one large lemon

⅔ cup water

4 egg yolks

1 egg

2 tablespoons melted butter

MERINGUE:

4 egg whites

3 tablespoons sugar

FOR THE CRUST: Place flour and salt in a large, shallow mixing bowl, and stir well to mix. Add lard and cut in with a pastry blender or knives until texture is that of uncooked oatmeal. Add water, a few drops at a time, mixing briskly with a fork until dough holds together. Turn out on a lightly floured board and roll into a thick circle about 11 inches in diameter. Fit pastry into an 8-inch pie pan, roll overhang under even with rim and crimp.

FOR THE FILLING: Mix sugar, cornstarch, and salt; stir in lemon rind, lemon juice, and water. Add egg yolks, one at a time, beating well after each addition. Add the whole egg and beat well. Blend in melted butter. Pour mixture into unbaked pie shell and bake in a preheated oven at 325 degrees for 30 to 35 minutes, until bubbly and begins to thicken. Remove from oven and let stand for 10 minutes. Raise oven temperature to 450 degrees.

FOR THE MERINGUE: Beat egg whites until frothy; continue beating, adding sugar gradually, until meringue peaks softly. Spread gently over lemon filling, making sure meringue touches crimped edges of crust all around. Return to oven and bake 2–3 minutes until meringue is tipped with brown. Cool to room temperature before cutting.

*I*n July of 1840, McConnel, Bunn & Co. opened for business in Springfield. Two years later, Jacob Bunn bought the business and operated it as a wholesale and retail grocery store and changed the name to J. Bunn & Co. According to their 1849–1850 ledger, Mary Lincoln purchased some of the family's grocery staples from the store.

An engraving of Lincoln and his son, Tad, done from a photograph by Matthew Brady. The book the father and son are leafing through is a photo album that Brady had in his studio.

No family portrait was ever done of the Lincolns. This engraving is an artist's rendering done in 1865, based on the above Brady photograph. Son Robert stands behind his parents. Wanting to portray all of the President's children, the artist included a portrait (seen in the upper right corner) of son Willie, who had died in February 1862. (Donna McCreary collection)

Washington, D.C.

❦✱❦

The President's House
(Abe's Antiques of Gettysburg)

❦✱❦

On November 6, 1860, the Lincoln family waited, as did the nation, as the election returns came in. Mary waited at home while Mr. Lincoln went to the room reserved for him at the State House. That evening they attend a special supper hosted by the Republican ladies held at Watson's Confectionery. Lincoln's campaign supporters and friends crowded into the capitol to hear the election returns. Later in the evening, Lincoln and a group of friends were in the telegraph office receiving the news of the returns. Lyman Trumbull was one of the first to say, "If we get New York that settles it." The man receiving the telegram became very excited as the message arrived saying that New York had gone Republican.

Lincoln, who had been standing in the doorway when the first shout went up, realized the nation was in crisis and that his responsibilities would be great. Crowd members began shouting, throwing up their hats, and slapping one another on the back. The Rail Splitter had won.

Lincoln turned to his friend Trumbull and said, "I guess I'll go down and tell Mary about it." And with that, he turned and headed towards the home on Eighth and Jackson. Mary, while awaiting the news, had fallen asleep. She was confident her husband would be elected. Somewhere between her dreams and reality she knew her confidence had been rewarded. Lincoln relayed the story of telling Mary the good news to the editor of *The Independent*, Henry C. Bowen:

> *I told my wife to go to bed, as probably I should not be back before midnight. . . . On my arrival I went to my bedroom and found my wife sound asleep. I gently touched her shoulder and said, "Mary"; she made no answer. I spoke again, a little louder, saying, "Mary, Mary! we are elected!"*

Lincoln's Table

After arriving in Washington, D.C., the Lincoln family stayed at Willard's Hotel until after the inauguration on March 4, 1861. They remained there for ten days, in Room 6. Dining in their room, and treating guests to champagne and cigars, they received a total bill of $773.75. Despite the cheers, toasts, and celebration of Lincoln becoming the new President, the city and the nation was preparing for war. Everyone experienced change. Even Willard's Hotel prepared by "furling all sails for the storm. The dining table shorn of cartes, and the tea table reduced to the severe simplicity of pound cake." It was at Willard's that the inaugural luncheon was served after the ceremonies at the Capitol. Lincoln himself planned the simple menu which was served that afternoon. After lunch, the family went directly to the Executive Mansion.

❧

Lincoln's Inaugural Luncheon

Mock Turtle Soup
Corned Beef and Cabbage
Parsley Potatoes
Blackberry Pie
Coffee

❧

Mock Turtle Soup

Cover 5 pounds of veal bones with 14 cups water. Bring to the boiling point. And the following ingredients, cover, and simmer for 3 ½ hours:

6	chopped celery ribs with leaves
5	coarsely cut carrots
1	cup chopped onion
2	cups canned tomatoes
1	small can (6 ounces) tomato paste
6	crushed peppercorns
1	tablespoon salt
6	whole cloves
2	bay leaves
½	teaspoon dried thyme

Remove bones and fat. In a greased skillet, sauté the following for five minutes:

2	minced cloves of garlic
2	pounds of ground beef
2	teaspoons salt

Add:

¼	teaspoon Worcestershire sauce
4	teaspoons sugar

Add meat to the soup stock. Bring to a boil, reduce heat, and simmer 30 minutes.

Blend together:

6	tablespoons of browned flour	*(flour that has been browned in meat grease, in a skillet. The residue from*
1	cup of cooled stock	*the ground beef can be used.)*

When this has thickened to form a paste, add it to the simmering soup. Simmer for five minutes more.

Add:

2   thinly sliced lemons
1   set of chopped parboiled calf's brains*

Reheat, but do not bring to a boil. Serve the soup garnished with:

3   sliced hard-boiled eggs

(* In Lincoln's era, a calf's head could be purchased. Instead of veal bones to make the soup stock, the calf's head was boiled, thus cooking the brains as well as making the stock. Leftover meat was picked off the bones, and the skull was then broken open to remove the cooked brains.)

Corned Beef and Cabbage

(Historic version)

Choose the thick end of a flank of beef, but do not let it be too fat. Let it lie in salt, and pickle for a week to ten days.

Sufficiently salt the meat. Prepare the following seasonings:

One handful of parsley,
        chopped fine
Thyme
Marjoram
Basil
Pepper
Sage (optional)
Allspice (optional)

Mix all well together, and cove the entire inside of the beef with the seasonings.

Roll the meat up tightly, then roll it in a clean cloth. Bind with a strong string and tie it close at the ends.

Boil it gently for three to four hours, and when cooked, take it up. Tie the ends again, quite close to the meat, and place it between two dishes with a heavy weight at the top. When it is cold, remove the cloth.

After carefully preparing the meat, it can be stored in a refrigerator for a couple of days before using.

Place meat in a deep pan. Cut green cabbage into wedges and place around meat. Cook slowly, until cabbage is tender and meat is thoroughly heated.

Corned Beef and Cabbage

(Modern version, serves 4–6.)

1	5-pound joint of corned beef
2	large onions
2	large carrots
4	potatoes
1	large cabbage
	Bay leaf
	Freshly ground black pepper

Quarter the cabbage and set aside. Peel and slice the other vegetables. Place meat in a pan with enough water to cover the meat; bring to a boil. Skim foam off the surface, add the onions, carrots, potatoes, bay leaf, and pepper and simmer gently for 90 minutes. Add the cabbage and cook for another 30 minutes. Serve the meat surrounded by the vegetables with additional potatoes.

Parsley Potatoes

6	medium sized potatoes, washed and peeled
3	tablespoons butter
3	tablespoons flour
1	cup milk
1	tablespoon parsley
	Salt and pepper to taste

Boil potatoes until tender. Drain and place in casserole dish. Melt butter in a sauce pan. Add flour and milk. Stir so flour does not lump and mixture thickens. Add parsley, salt, and pepper. Pour over potatoes. Bake in preheated 350 degree oven for 15 minutes or until hot and milk begins to bubble.

Blackberry Pie

(for an 8-inch pie)

Pastry for an 8-inch
double-crust pie
2   cups blackberries
3   tablespoons flour
¾   cup sugar
2   tablespoons butter

Preheat oven to 450 degrees. Line pie pan with unbaked pie shell. Mix together all ingredients except butter. Place berries in pie pan. Dot with butter. Either bake with a cover crust that has been vented, or with a lattice top crust. Bake for 10 minutes. Lower temperature to 375 degrees and bake for another 20–25 minutes, or till golden brown.

(*Above*) The President's "summer White House," the Soldier's Home (as it looked about 1900), had a country rusticity that contrasted with the elegant formality of the White House in Washington, D.C. (*below*). (Abe's Antiques of Gettysburg)

PRESIDENT'S HOUSE
WASHINGTON, D.C.

White House Beverages

Sarah Josepha Hale wrote in *The Good Housekeeper* that there was one rule of domestic living that women should never violate: "Never make any preparation of which alcohol forms a part for family use!" Mrs. Hale was so adamant about her position concerning alcohol that she did not allow any recipes using it in her cookbook or her domestic writings.

Mary Lincoln followed this advice as a matron in Springfield. Lincoln did not drink strong liquor. She had an older brother whose life had been destroyed by his love affair with whiskey—she was not going to serve it in her home. Even on that special night when gentlemen came to discuss being the Republican presidential nominee with Lincoln, ice water was the chosen beverage.

In the White House, Mary took a slightly different stand on the temperance issue. Although neither she nor her husband themselves partook of alcoholic beverages, on rare occasions alcohol was served. The temperance groups attacked Mary Lincoln viciously for her "lenience."

The Lincolns were given countless bottles of imported wines, bourbons, and fine liquors. They made sure that every bottle was used and did not go to waste. Gifts of alcohol were boxed and given to the military hospitals in the Washington, D.C., area for medicinal purposes. On occasion, Mary made the deliveries to the hospital herself.

Mary Lincoln's Champagne Punch

(Makes 64 four-ounce servings)

3   quarts champagne
2   quarts sauterne
3   quarts soda water
1   gill (4 ounces) Curacao
    Fresh fruit, such as
      strawberries,
      raspberries, peaches, or
      other fruit that is in
      season

At serving time, place a large chunk of ice in a punch bowl. Mix the liquors in another bowl, and pour into the punch bowl. Add fresh fruit to the punch and use a few pieces of fruit to adorn the top of the punch bowl.

Raspberry Shrub

(Historic 1860s version)

Pick berries when fully ripe and juicy. Place in an earthen pot which must be set into an iron pot of water. Bring the water to a boil, but take care than none of it gets into the fruit.

When the juice is extracted from the fruit, pour into a bag made of rather thick cloth which will permit the juice to pass through, but not the pulp or seeds.

Sweeten the juice to taste.

When the juice becomes perfectly clear, place a gill (4 ounces) of brandy into each bottle before pouring the juice in the bottle. Cork the bottle. Cover the cork with rosin. It will keep all summer in a cool dry place.

Raspberry Shrub

(Modern version, non-alcoholic. Makes 24 four-ounce servings)

4	packages of frozen raspberries
1	can frozen lemonade concentrate
2	quarts of ginger ale

Cook the raspberries in a saucepan over low heat for 10 minutes. Rub berries through a strainer with a wooden spoon. Cool. Add lemonade concentrate; stir in ginger ale. Serve immediately with crushed ice.

Variation: If alcohol is desired, pour a small amount of brandy or curaçao in the bottom of each cup or glass before adding the crushed ice.

White House Appetizers

❧

Buttered Crab on Remekins

Slices of hard cheese such as
cheddar
Pieces of toasted bread
Crab meat
Butter

Place butter on one side of the toasted bread, and a slice of hard cheese on the other side. Grill until cheese starts to melt. Remove from the grill and spread the crab meat over the cheese. Re-grill to heat and brown the crab meat.

If desired, the toasted bread can be cut with a round cookie cutter. Then lay in a shallow muffin tray so that each remekin forms a slight hollow into which the crab can be spooned prior to the final grilling.

Tomato Bisque

2 ¼ cups chopped tomatoes
1 teaspoon sugar
3 tablespoons butter
1 bay leaf
¼ cup chopped fresh parsley
1 cup dry bread crumbs
4 cups milk (low-fat milk can be used)
1 small onion, chopped
Salt and pepper to taste

In a large pot, add water to just to cover the bottom of the pan. Add tomatoes and sugar and cook over medium heat for 20 minutes, or until tomatoes are tender.

In a small saucepan, melt the butter and sauté the onion until translucent. Add the onion mixture, bay leaf, and parsley to the tomatoes and cook for 5 minutes. Remove the bay leaf and discard. Puree the tomato and onion mixture. Return the mixture to the soup pot.

In a large saucepan, combine the bread crumbs and the milk; heat just to scalding. Add the milk mixture to the tomato mixture and stir well. Add salt and pepper to taste, and serve.

Paté de Foie Poulet

1	pound chicken livers
1 ¼	cups chicken broth
¼	medium onion
⅛	teaspoon rosemary
¼	cup softened butter
1	clove garlic (optional)
6	slices bacon, fried crisp
¼	teaspoon salt
⅛	teaspoon pepper
¼	teaspoon dry mustard

Simmer chicken livers in chicken broth for 15 minutes. Remove livers from broth, and reserve ¼ cup of the liquid. Process all ingredients except reserved broth and seasonings through a food mill; place in a bowl, add broth and seasonings and blend until well mixed. Place in a container and chill for at least 24 hours.

(Note: The modern cook may wish to combine these ingredients in a blender or food processor to save time.)

Aspic and Tongue

1	tongue
	Onions
	Green bell peppers
¼	cup cherry juice
	Aspic*

Preheat oven to 200 degrees. Place tongue in a pan with water with onions and peppers and bake for six hours. Add cherry juice and continue cooking until tongue is tender. Let cool, slice, and arrange on a cool tray; cover with aspic and serve.

(* *Aspic is clear gelatin made from meat. Place the meat in two quarts of cold water. Bring to a boil, skim foam from the top, then reduce heat and simmer for six hours. Remove meat, strain the broth into a deep dish, and refrigerate for at least 24 hours. Remove the fat from the top, bring broth to a boil, and reduce to about one quart. For all practical, modern purposes, unflavored gelatin is quicker, easier, and produces almost the same results. Prepare it with a meat stock instead of water.*)

Smoked Venison with Applesauce

Smoke a venison roast in a smoker with the meat over a pan of water and fruit juice that is available as per season. Pack fruit around the meat to keep it moist. Use a good fruit wood or hickory wood for the smoke. Keep the pan from going dry by adding water whenever needed. When the meat is judged to be cooked, slice it and let it cool. Serve the venison cold with applesauce in small portions.

Sicilian Sorbet

	Fresh peaches
2	cups orange juice
1	cup sugar
2	tablespoons lemon juice

Press the peaches through a sieve. Add sugar and juices. Freeze and serve.

Mushroom Soup

1 quart water
1 pound fresh mushrooms
3 slices bacon, diced
2 tablespoons flour
2 small onion
  Juice from one can of sauerkraut (about ¼ cup)
  Salt and pepper to taste

Cook mushrooms in 1 quart water until tender. Drain; reserve liquid.

Fry bacon until partially done. Add flour; cook until lightly browned. Add onion and sauté, stirring constantly, for five minutes.

Combine sauerkraut juice with reserved mushroom liquid. Season with salt and pepper. Bring to a boil. Add ½ cup of the sauerkraut-mushroom juice mixture to bacon mixture gradually. Simmer, stirring constantly, until mixture is smooth. Add remaining liquid gradually. Add mushrooms and simmer, stirring, until well blended and heated through.

White House Breads

Caraway Bread

2   packages of yeast
¾   cup warm water
1 ¼   cups buttermilk or sour
          milk
5   cups flour (about)
¼   cup shortening
2   tablespoons sugar
2   teaspoons baking powder
2   teaspoons salt
1   tablespoon caraway seeds
       Soft butter

Dissolve yeast in warm water in a large bowl. Add buttermilk, 2 ½ cups flour, shortening, sugar, baking powder, salt, and caraway seeds. Blend for 30 seconds at low speed with an electric mixer, or for about 1 minute by hand. Scrap sides and bottom of the bowl while mixing. Beat for two minutes at medium speed with an electric mixer, or beat rigorously by hand. Stir in remaining flour by hand. Dough should be soft and slightly sticky.

Turn dough onto heavily floured board; knead well. Roll dough to 18 x 9-inch rectangle. Roll up from short side as for jelly roll; press each end to seal. Fold ends under loaf. Place seam-side down in a greased bread pan; brush loaf lightly with butter. Let rise for 1 hour, or until double in bulk. Bake at 375 degrees for 45 minutes or until bread tests done.

Corn Bread

(makes 6 pieces)

¾   cup sifted flour
1 ¼   cups corn meal
4   teaspoons baking powder
1   teaspoon salt
2   tablespoons sugar
2   eggs, well beaten
1 ¼   cups milk
¼   cup melted butter

Combine dry ingredients. Combine eggs and milk and add to flour mixture, stirring until well mixed. Add melted butter. Turn into a greased, shallow pan, or into corn muffin tins. Bake at 400 degrees for 30 minutes.

(Note: Sugar may be omitted if desired.)

White House Vegetables

❦

Weisskohl mit Speck *(Cabbage with Bacon)*

(serves 6)

1	medium head of white cabbage (about 1 ½ pounds) finely shredded
4	slices bacon
¼	cup vinegar
1	teaspoon sugar
½	teaspoon dry mustard
¼	teaspoon salt
⅛	teaspoon pepper
5	green onions with tops, sliced (about ½ cup)

Cover cabbage with boiling water in a 4-quart bowl. Let stand for 10 minutes; drain. Cook bacon in a large skillet until crisp. Remove from heat. Crumble the bacon into small pieces. Add vinegar, sugar, mustard, salt and pepper; heat thoroughly over medium heat. Add the cabbage and onions. Toss until cabbage is coated with the bacon mixture.

Delmonico's Restaurant was a favorite dining haunt of the President's when he was in New York City. During one visit Lincoln told the owner, Lorenzo Delmonico, "In my city of Washington there are many mansions, but alas, we have no cooks like yours."

Delmonico Potatoes

(serves 4)

6	potatoes, peeled and diced
4	tablespoons butter
4	tablespoons flour
1 ¾	cups cream
¾	grated white cheese
	Salt and pepper
	Handful of bread crumbs

In a large pan, boil the potatoes in lightly salted water until done. Drain and place the potatoes in a buttered baking dish. Melt the butter in a sauce pan over low heat. Blend in flour. Add cream. Cook, stirring constantly, until thickened. Add salt and pepper to taste. Pour sauce over the potatoes and mix. Cover with cheese. Dot with additional butter and bread crumbs. Bake for 20 minutes at 400 degrees.

Maple Glazed Turnips

1	pound sliced young turnips
3	tablespoons brown sugar
	Maple syrup
	Butter

Steam turnips in a small among of water in a steamer for 20 minutes or until tender. Drain. Season with brown sugar, maple syrup, and butter. Toss lightly

White House Entrees

❧

Filet of Beef

1	small beef shoulder, rump, or chuck roast
1	tablespoon Worcestershire sauce
1	cup red wine
	Pepper to taste
¼	teaspoon tarragon
¼	teaspoon rosemary
1	small onion, sliced

Preheat oven to 300 degrees. Place beef in a lidded roasting pan. Mix all other ingredients together and pour over the top of the beef. Cover and roast until meat is done, turning occasionally. (Roasting time will vary, depending on the size of the roast.)

The President's Chaire

(serves 6–8)

1	chicken (3 to 3 ½ pounds)
1	cup water
¼	cup lemon juice
1	onion, chopped
	Salt and pepper to taste
3	tablespoons prepared mustard
2	tablespoons brown sugar
2	teaspoons fat
½	cup chopped celery
1	cup catsup
2	tablespoons vinegar

Cut chicken into serving pieces. Brown in hot fat in a skillet. Remove chicken pieces and place in a casserole dish. Add chopped onion to fat and brown lightly. Add remaining ingredients and simmer for 30 minutes. Pour over browned chicken in the casserole. Cover casserole with a dome shaped lid and bake at 350 degrees for one hour.

Wine Glazed Ham

1	10-pound ham
	Whole cloves
2 ½	cups white wine
1	cup honey
1	cup brown sugar, packed

Remove rind from ham, leaving a thin layer of fat. Score the fat. Stud with cloves. Place, fat side up, in a roaster. Pour white wine over the ham. Spread honey over top; sprinkle with brown sugar. Bake at 300 degrees for 1 hour. Cover; bake for 3 hours longer or until ham is tender, basting frequently.

Roast Goose with Apricot Stuffing

2 ¼ cups cooked unsweetened
     apricots
2   cups fresh bread crumbs
¼   cups butter, melted
¼   cup slivered, toasted
     almonds
     Pepper to taste
2   cups cracker crumbs
¼   cup minced celery
1 ¼ teaspoons salt
1   goose

Cut apricots into small pieces. Add remaining ingredients, and stir well.

Preheat oven to 375 degrees. Fill goose with Apricot Stuffing. Truss and place breast down in a large roasting pan. Pour 2 cups of boiling water over the goose and cover the pan with lid. Bake 30 minutes. Turn goose breast up and prick with a fork in inconspicuous places about the legs and wings, so that the fat will run out. Reduce heat to 300 degrees and roast for 2 to 2 ¼ hours, adding more water as necessary. Remove lid and roast uncovered for another 15 minutes to brown.

White House Desserts

Berries in Filled Dough

Pie pastry dough

FILLING:

1	cup butter
4	eggs
2	cups sugar
1	teaspoon vanilla

TOPPING:

	Raspberries and blueberries
2	cups whipped cream
	Powdered sugar

FOR THE PASTRY: Roll pastry dough thinly and cut into circles to fit into individual baking cups.

FOR THE FILLING: Preheat oven to 375 degrees. Combine ingredients and pour into pastry cups. Bake for 10 minutes or until light brown.

FOR THE TOPPING: Remove pastries from cups. Top with berries, powdered sugar and whipped cream.

Chocolate Pie

MERINGUE CRUST:

3 egg whites

¼ teaspoon cream of tarter

¾ cup sugar

FILLING:

1 cup butter

4 eggs

2 cups sugar

1 teaspoon vanilla

HOT FUDGE SAUCE:

(makes 1–1 ¾ cups)

¾ cup sugar

½ cup cocoa

1 5-ounce can evaporated
milk

⅓ cup light corn syrup

⅓ cup butter

1 teaspoon vanilla extract

FOR THE CRUST: Beat egg whites until soft peaks form. Slowly add other ingredients. Beat until it forms stiff peaks as for a meringue. Gentle spoon into pie pan. Bake at 275 degrees for one hour.

FOR THE FILLING: Combine ingredients and beat for 20 minutes. Gently pour into meringue crust. Bake at 375 degrees for 10 minutes. Garnish with hot fudge sauce.

FOR THE SAUCE: Combine sugar and cocoa in a medium saucepan. Stir in evaporated milk and corn syrup. Cook over medium heat, stirring constantly until the mixture boils. Boil for 1 minute. Remove from heat. Stir in butter and vanilla. Serve warm over above pie or other desserts.

A receipt book of a Washington baker records that President Lincoln was a steady customer for this unusually rich pecan pie.

Molasses Pecan Pie

(Makes one 8-inch pie, serves 6–8)

3	eggs
¾	cups unsulphured molasses
¾	cup white corn syrup
1	teaspoon vanilla extract
1	tablespoon flour
2	tablespoons melted butter
⅛	teaspoon salt
1	cup chopped pecans
1	unbaked 8-inch pie shell

Preheat oven to 375 degrees. Beat eggs until light and frothy. Add melted butter; mix well. Add molasses, white corn syrup, salt, and vanilla. Mix well. Coat the pecans with the flour; then add floured nuts to the egg-butter mixture. Mix thoroughly and pour into pie shell. Bake for 40 minutes or until the filling sets and becomes firm.

As a child in New Hampshire, nineteenth-century author Sarah Josepha Hale and her family had celebrated Thanksgiving Day, a common practice only in some states. She began a lifelong crusade to have Thanksgiving Day declared a national holiday. In 1863, when she was seventy-five years old, President Abraham Lincoln made her dream a reality. He wrote:

> . . . *invite my fellow citizens in every part of the United States, and also those who are at sea, or who are sojourning in foreign lands, to set apart and observe the last Thursday of November next as a day of thanksgiving and praise to our Beneficent Father.*

Thanksgiving Pumpkin Pie

1 ½   cups cooked pumpkin
1 ½   cups scalded milk
2   tablespoons butter
½   teaspoon salt
1   teaspoon cinnamon
3   eggs, separated
1   cup sugar
½   teaspoon ginger
¼   teaspoon nutmeg
1   unbaked 9-inch pie shell

Strain the cooked pumpkin. Lightly beat the egg yolks and add to the pumpkin.

Melt butter in hot milk. Add scalded milk to pumpkin mixture. Mix well. Add sugar, salt, ginger, cinnamon, and nutmeg. Mix thoroughly.

Beat egg whites until stiff peaks form. Carefully fold egg whites into pumpkin mixture. Pour mixture into unbaked pie shell. Bake in a preheated 450 degree oven for 10 minutes. Reduce heat to 350 degrees and bake for 20–25 minutes longer. When a knife can be inserted into the filling and it comes out clean, the pie is done.

Christmas Pumpkin Pie

(Makes two 9-inch pies)

10   eggs
4   cups cooked, strained
     pumpkin
2   cups dark brown sugar
1   teaspoon mace
1   tablespoon brandy
½   teaspoon nutmeg
1   teaspoon cinnamon
1 ¼ quarts whole milk
2   unbaked 9-inch pie shells

Separate the eggs. Beat the 10 egg yolks and combine with the pumpkin in a large bowl. Add dark brown sugar and spices. Mix well. Add brandy. Mix again. Slowly add the milk, beating well as it is added.

Beat the 10 egg whites until stiff peaks form. Fold into the pumpkin mixture.

Pour mixture into pie shells. Bake for 20 minutes in preheated 425 degree oven. Reduce heat to 325 degrees and bake another 25 minutes or until center is firm.

The First Lady
(Donna McCreary collection)

Menu for a White House Ball

February 5, 1862

Decorations and Candy Ornaments included:

A five-foot-high vase, filled with natural flowers, wreaths of which
    gracefully vined about the sides and base of the vase

A United States steam frigate of forty guns, with all sail set, and the
    flag of the Union flying at the main

A representation of the Hermitage

A Warrior's helmet, supported by Cupids

A Chinese pagoda

Double cornucopias, resting upon a shell, supported by mermaids,
    surmounted by a crystal star

A rustic pavilion

The Goddess of Liberty

A magnificent candelabra, surmounted by an elegant vase of flowers
    and surrounded by tropical fruits and birds, tastefully arranged and
    sustained by kneeling Cupids

A basket, laden with flowers and fruits, mounted on a pedestal
    supported by swans

Four bee hives

A Swiss cottage in sugar and cake

A large fort, named Fort Pickens, made of cake and sugared. The inside
    was filled with quails, candied

Lincoln's Table

The menu included:

Stewed Oysters
Scalloped Oysters
Boned Turkey
Paté de Foie Gras
Aspic of Torgul
Patti-Gillets, à la Fanisanz
Chicken Salad, à la Parisenne
Filet of Beef
Stuffed Turkey with Truffles
Quails
Canvas Back Ducks
Charlotte Russe, à la Parisenne
Chateaubriand

Chocolate Bavarian
Jelly Compettes
Fruit Glacé
Bon-Bons
Orange Glacé
Biscuit Glacé
Fancy Cakes
Rich Mottoes
Flower Mottoes
Sandwiches
Fruit and Grapes
Meringues

The East Ballroom as it
appeared during Lincoln's time.
(Abe's Antiques of Gettysburg)

Lincoln's Table

BILL OF FARE
of the
Presidential Inauguration Ball
in the
CITY OF WASHINGTON, D.C.
On the 6th of March 1865.

Oyster Stew ....
Terrapin Stew ....
Oysters, pickled ....

BEEF,

Roast Beef ....
Filet of Beef ....
Beef à la mode ....
Beef à l'anglais ....

VEAL,

Leg of Veal ....
Fricandeau ....
Veal Malakoff...

POULTRY,

Roast Turkey ....
Boned Turkey ....
Breast Chicken ....
Grouse, boned and roast ....

GAME,

Pheasant ....
Quail ....
Venison ....

PATETES,

Patète of Duck en gelee
Patète de Foie gras ....

SMOKED,

Ham ....
Tongue en gelée ....
do plain ....

SALADES,

Chicken ....
Lobster ....

ORNAMENTAL PYRAMIDES,

Nougate ....
Orange ....
Caramel with Fancy Cream Candy ....
Cocoanut ....
Macaroon ....

Croquant ....
Chocolates ....
Trea Cakes ....

CAKES AND TARTS,

Almond Sponge ....
Belle Alliance ....
Dame Blanche ....
Macaroon Tart ....
Tart à la Nelson ....
Tart à l'Orleans ....
do à la Portugaise ....
do à la Vienne ....
Pound Cake ....
Sponge Cake ....
Lady Cake ....
Fancy small cakes ....

JELLIES AND CREAMS,

Calf's foot and Wine Jelly
Charlotte à la Russe
do du Vanilla ....
Blanc Mangue ....
Crème Neapolitano ....
do à la Nelson ....
do Chateaubriand ....
do à la Smyrna ....
do à la Nesselrode ....
Bombe à la Vanilla ....

ICE CREAM,

Vanilla ....
Lemon ....
White Coffee ....
Chocolate ....
Burnt Almond ....
Maraschino ....

FRUIT ICES,

Strawberry ....
Orange ....
Lemon ....

DESSERT,

Grapes, Almonds, Raisins, &c

Coffee and Chocolate

Furnished by G. A. BALZER, Confectioners,
Cor. 9th & D Sts, Washington, D.C.

White House Menu

Champagne punch and Raspberry Shrub

Buttered Crab on Remekins

Tomato Bisque

Aspic of Tongue

Paté de Foie Poulet

Smoked Venison

Fruit Sorbet

Filet of Beef

Roast Goose with Apricot Stuffing

Delmonico Potatoes

Maple Glazed Turnips

Fruit

Coffee and Tea

Dessert Cakes and Confections

Napoleon Brandy and Sherry

White House Menu

Champagne Punch and Raspberry Shrub

Scalloped Oysters

Mushroom Soup

Aspic of Tongue

Paté de Foie Poulet

Mushroom stuffed Turkey

Sicilian Sorbet

Fillet of Beef and Wine Glazed Ham

Delmonico Potatoes

Weisskohl mit Speck

Fruit

Coffee and Tea

Dessert cakes and Confections

The last photograph of Abraham Lincoln was taken by subterfuge on March 6, 1865, two days after Lincoln gave his second inaugural address. Henry F. Warren, a photographer unknown to the President, managed to get into the White House grounds, where he found young Tad Lincoln and offered to photograph the child on his pony if he would get his father to pose also. The ruse was successful, and Tad coaxed his father to come out on the balcony for the photographer. It is speculated that Lincoln's annoyance with Warren's trick was the cause of his stern expression—or perhaps it was the wind that whipped his hair and possibly stung his eyes. Abraham Lincoln was assassinated less than six weeks later.

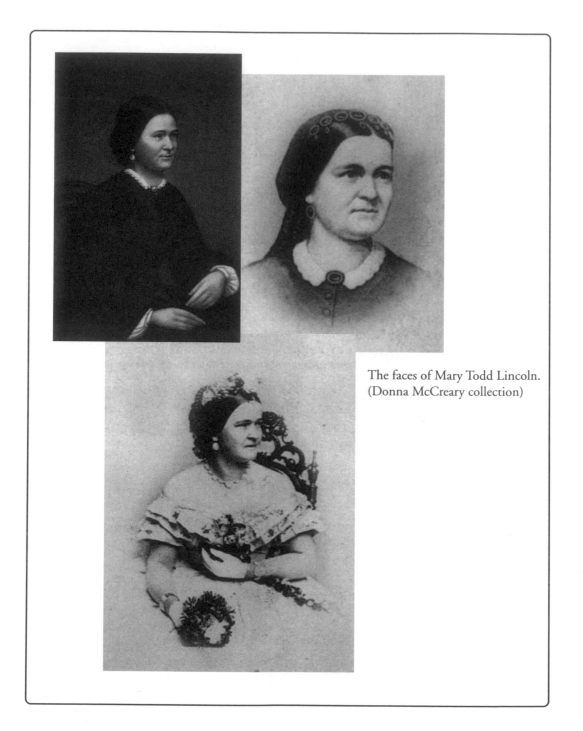

The faces of Mary Todd Lincoln.
(Donna McCreary collection)

Author Donna McCreary with fellow Association of
Lincoln Presenters member Patrick McCreary (no
relation). Both are members of the board of directors of
the association.

Bibliography

BOOKS

American Heritage, Inc. *American Heritage Cookbook*. American Heritage Publishing, 1964.

Anderson, Jean. *Recipes from America's Restored Villages*. New York: Doubleday and Co., 1975.

Barnes, Bertha. *Antique Cook Book*. Harlan, Kentucky: Durham Printing and Offset, 1974.

Betty Crocker's Cookbook. New York: Prentice Hall,1991.

Cannon, Poppy, and Patricia Brooks. *The President's Cookbook*. Funk and Wagnalls, 1968.

Conway, W. Fred. *Young Abe Lincoln: His Teenage Years in Indiana*. New Albany, IN: FBH Publishers, 1992.

Donald, David Herbert. *Lincoln*. New York: Simon & Schuster, 1995.

Editors of Favorite Recipes Press. *The Illustrated Encyclopedia of American Cooking*. Nashville, TN: Southwestern Company, 1992.

Ervin, Janet Halliday. *The White House Cookbook*. Chicago: Follett Publishing, 1964.

Flexner, Marion. W. *Out of Kentucky Kitchens*. Lexington: University Press of Kentucky, 1989.

French, Marian. *Lincoln Heritage Trail Cookbook*. Williamsburg, VA: Bi-Cast Publishers, 1992–94.

Hale, Sarah Josepha. *Early American Cookery: The Good Housekeeper, 1841* (reprint). New York: Dover Publications, Inc., 1996.

Haller, Henry. *The White House Family Cookbook*. New York: Random House, 1987.

Holzer, Harold, ed. *Lincoln As I Knew Him*. Chapel Hill: Algonquin Books of Chapel Hill, 1999.

Jones, Robert. *The Presidents Own White House Cookbook*. Chicago: Culinary Arts Institute, 1973.

Miers, Earl Schenck, and William E. Baringer, eds. *Lincoln Day by Day: A Chronology, 1809–1865*. Vol. I, 1809–1848. Dayton: Morningside, 1991.

Randall, Ruth Painter. *Mary Lincoln, Biography of a Marriage*. Boston: Little, Brown and Company, 1953.

Randolph, Mary. *The Virginia Housewife, or Methodical Cook* (reprint). New York: Dover Publishers, Inc., 1993.

Smith, Myrtle Ellison. *Civil War Cookbook.* Harogate, TN: Lincoln Memorial University.

Spaulding, Lily May, and John Spaulding, eds. *Civil War Recipes: Receipts from the Pages of Godey's Lady's Book.* Lexington: University Press of Kentucky, 1999.

Stoner, Carol Hupping, ed.*Stocking Up: How To Preserve the Foods You Grow Naturally.* Rodale Press, 1977.

Wallace, Richard, and Maire Pinak Carr. *The Willard Hotel: An Illustrated History.* Carr and Carr, 1984.

Ziemann, Hugo, and Mrs. F. L. Gillette. *The White House Cookbook.*Werner, 1894.

MANUSCRIPTS

Chicago Historical Society:
> *Chicago Tribune* (Special to the *New York Herald*) February 5, 1862
> *Chicago Tribune* (Special to the *New York Tribune*) February 10, 1862
> Robert Todd Lincoln Collection, Folder 7 of 11

Kentucky Historical Society, Frankfort, Kentucky:
> Helm Family Papers

King Library, University of Kentucky, Lexington, Kentucky:
> William Townsend Collection, Helm Family Papers

HISTORICAL SITE SOURCES

The staff of Farmington Historic Home, Louisville, Kentucky.

The staff of Abraham Lincoln Birthplace National Historic Site, Hodgenville, Kentucky.

Dusty Schultz and the staff of Lincoln Boyhood National Historic Site, Lincoln City, Indiana.

Judy Winkleman of Linclon Home National Historic Site, Springfield, Illinois.

Kathy Tabb of Mary Todd Lincoln Home, Lexington, Kentucky.

Kristina Messner of Willard's Intercontinental Hotel, Washington, D.C.

Index

Lincoln's Table